Walt Disney's Comics and Stories
No. 649, October 2004
Published monthly by Gemstone Publishing,
© 2004 Disney Enterprises, Inc., except where noted.
All rights reserved. Nothing contained herein may be reproduced
without the written permission of Disney Enterprises, Inc.,
Burbank, CA., or other copyright holders.

ISBN 0-911903-50-X

GET OUT OF TOWN, UNCA DONALD! YOU COULDN'T LUG AROUND A **POUND** OF CANDY WITHOUT COLLAPSING FROM EXHAUSTION!

OH, YEAH?

LISTEN, PIPSQUEAKS, IF I PUT MY MIND TO IT, I COULD COME HOME WITH A **THOUSAND** POUNDS OF CANDY AND NOT EVEN WRINKLE MY COSTUME!

WE'LL CALL YOUR BLUFF, UNCA DONALD!

LET'S HAVE A TRICK OR TREATING CONTEST! YOU AGAINST US, AND WHICHEVER SIDE COMES HOME WITH THE **MOST** CANDY WINS!

YOU'RE ON! WHAT'S THE FORFEIT GOING TO BE THIS TIME?

THE **LOSER** GIVES ALL OF HIS CANDY TO THE WINNERS!

WHO'LL BE **US**!

AND SO...

THIS OLD COSTUME I WORE WHEN I WAS A TAMALE SALESMAN IN LA JOLLA HAS SURE COME IN HANDY TONIGHT!

IT WON'T BEAT OUT A GHOST, A PIRATE, AND A CLOWN, UNCA DONALD!

WE'LL SEE, WISE GUYS! HERE'S THE FIRST HOUSE!

I DON'T KNOW WHY THE LAW ALLOWS SOREHEADS LIKE THAT LOOSE ON HALLOWEEN! I'D BETTER SCORE PRETTY SOON! THE BOYS ARE RAKING IN THE GOODIES HAND OVER FIST!

HERE YOU ARE, KIDS! A NICE BOX OF CHOCOLATE CREAMS FOR EACH OF YOU!

OBOY! THANK YOU, MA'AM!

AHEM!

YES, WELL, I SUPPOSE THERE'S ONE FOR YOU, TOO! BUT REALLY, YOUNG MAN, YOU ARE A BIT OLD FOR THIS SORT OF THING!

NOW I'M COOKIN'!

HERE YOU ARE, BOYS! THE BEST ROCK CANDY THIS SIDE OF KOKOMO!

TRICK OR TREAT, SIR! I LOVE ROCK CANDY!

OH, YEAH? WELL, PUNK, YOU CAN FORGET ABOUT THE CANDY...

... BUT YOU'RE WELCOME TO THE ROCK! HAW! HAW!

MY CHOCOLATE CREAMS!

THUD

THERE, A DASH OF INSTANT WOODCRAFT, AND I'M READY FOR THOSE GLOATING GOSSOONS!

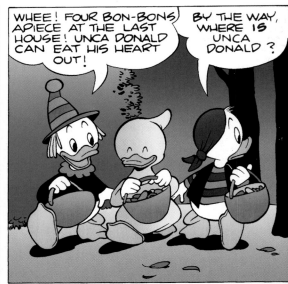

WHEE! FOUR BON-BONS APIECE AT THE LAST HOUSE! UNCA DONALD CAN EAT HIS HEART OUT!

BY THE WAY, WHERE IS UNCA DONALD?

SNAG

TRICK OR TREAT, BOYS! NYA-HA! HA!

HEY! THAT'S NOT FAIR!

COME BACK WITH MY CANDY!

NUTS TO YOU GUYS! THERE'S NOTHING IN THE RULES AGAINST—

TRICK OR TREAT! TRICK OR TREAT!

OOF

HA! I GET MY CANDY BACK AFTER ALL!

CRIME DOESN'T **PAY**, UNCA DONALD!

YEAH! YOU'RE SUPPOSED TO TRY AND WIN THE CONTEST BY BEING A TRICK OR TREATER—NOT A **SNEAK** THIEF!

JOOLS AN' MORE JOOLS! YAK! YAK! YAK! WOTTA HAUL FROM DESE RITZY DIGS! ROTTEN RALPH, YOUSE IS A PRODIGY OF PILFERAGE! IN FACT, IT'S ALARMIN' D'WAY I'M SO...

*A*ND SPEAKING OF SNEAK THIEVES...

DING DING DING DING...

ANUDDER ALARM! IT'S GETTIN' SO AN HONEST CROOK CAN'T TRUST **NOBODY** DESE DAYS!

OOGAH

COME ON, FEET! IT'S TIME TO PERAMBULATE WIT' ALACRITY! DIS PLACE'LL BE A REGULAR CLAMBAKE OF COPS IN ABOUT TEN SECONDS!

*M*EANWHILE...

THE BOYS ARE RIGHT! I'M GOING ABOUT THIS ALL **WRONG**!

TROUBLE IS—A GUY LIKE ME CAN'T GET ANYWHERE IN A TWO-BIT NEIGHBORHOOD LIKE THIS!

MY BOY, NEVER LET IT BE SAID THAT J. FUDGEGRIP TREACLE DOESN'T PAY HIS DEBTS! YOU'VE KEPT ME FROM THE TRULY **AWFUL** WRATH OF MY DEAR WIFE!

THANKS TO YOU, HER PRECIOUS GEGAWS ARE SAFE! NAME YOUR **REWARD!**

REWARD?

ANYTHING YOUR BLESSED HEART DESIRES, MR. DUCK! **ANYTHING AT ALL!**

WELL..THERE **IS** SOMETHING...

SOON THEREAFTER..

THAT'S QUITE A STORY, UNCA DONALD!

AND YOU'RE GOING TO GET A REWARD?

YEP!

WELL, REWARD OR NO REWARD— **WE** WIN THE CONTEST!

OUR BAGS ARE FULL!

AND YOURS IS **EMPTY** EXCEPT FOR SOME GOO. AT THE BOTTOM!

SORRY TO RAIN ON YOUR PARADE, BOYS! BUT AS IT TURNS OUT, **I'M** THE WINNER!

HOW? YOU DON'T HAVE ANY **CANDY!**

OH, BUT I **DO!** IN FACT, IT'S BEING DELIVERED RIGHT NOW!

???

MY REWARD! 25,000 POUNDS OF THE WORLD'S FINEST CHOCOLATE CREMES!

YOU SEE, BOYS, J. FUDGEGRIP TREACLE JUST HAPPENS TO BE THE OWNER OF DUCKBURG CHOCOLATE— THE BIGGEST CANDY COMPANY IN THE WORLD!

SO PAY UP!

I CAN'T BELIEVE IT! HALLOWEEN IS OVER AND WE'RE CANDILESS!

WELL, GUYS, I GUESS WE KNOW WHAT WE'RE GOING TO DO NEXT HALLOWEEN!

YEAH? WHAT?

WE'RE GOING TO KEEP OUR BIG, FAT MOUTHS SHUT ABOUT CONTESTS!

THE END

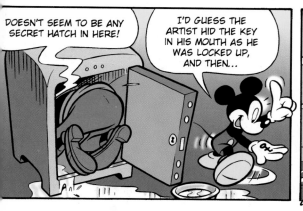

SOON...

THERE'S NO RESPECT ANY MORE, CRACKER! RICOTTA KNOWS THIS IS *OUR* TURF!

MUGWORT, LOOK!

IT MUST BE ONE OF RICOTTA'S BOYS!

WHAT AN AMATEUR! DRIVING AROUND WITH A STOLEN SAFE IN BROAD DAYLIGHT!

WELL, IF HE'S *THAT* STUPID, IT WON'T BE DIFFICULT TO NICK THE SAFE!

YEAH! RICOTTA NEEDS TO BE TAUGHT A LESSON!

OH NO! "FINGERS" LIVES ON THE SECOND FLOOR! I HAD ENOUGH TROUBLE DRAGGING THE SAFE OUT TO THE CAR AT *YOUR* PLACE, GOOFY!

GOOD DAY, SIR! YOU LOOK AS IF YOU NEED A HAND WITH THIS HEAVY PIECE OF FURNITURE!

YOU BET I DO!

YOU JUST HOLD THE DOOR, SIR! MY FRIEND AND I WILL BE HAPPY TO CARRY YOUR CUPBOARD FOR YOU!

GEE, THANKS!

OKAY, YOU CAN...

HEY!

⇥SNORT!⇤ I TOLD YA HE WAS AN AMATEUR!

STOP! COME BACK WITH MY SAFE!

SOME STUPID PICNIC WITH OLD COLLEAGUES, HE SAID! BUT IF ANYONE CAN OPEN THIS SAFE, IT'S "CAN-OPENER"!

THERE'S A TRUCK COMING, RICO!

NOW SOME *OTHER* CROOKS HAVE GOT THE SAFE! BUT I'M GONNA GET IT BACK!

~GASP!~

OMIGOSH! I BRAKED TOO HARD!

SCREEECH!

CRASH!

JUMP, BOSS!

OOF! HOPE THAT DIDN'T HURT TOO MUCH, GOOFY!

THONK!

NOW WE'VE GOTTA FIND "FINGERS"!

MUST BE ONE OF MUGWORT'S MEN! DOESN'T HE KNOW THIS IS *OUR* TURF?

VROOM!

MEANWHILE, JUST AROUND THE CORNER...

DARN IT! A FLAT TIRE, ONE BLOCK FROM HOME!

I'LL GET THE JACK, MUGWORT!

~GASP!~ THAT GUY'S DRIVING TOO FAST!

UH-OH!

SCREEECH!

HEY! WH-WHAT'S HAPPENING?

THONK!

SPLASH!

I FORGOT TO MENTION THE BRAKES, MICKEY! SOMETIMES THEY LOCK SOLID, SOMETIMES THEY JUST DON'T WORK!

GOOFY'S DOWN THERE, "FINGERS"! WE GOTTA GET HIM UP!

WELL, THAT'S WHAT MICKEY THINKS! BUT WE KNOW WHERE GOOFY REALLY IS...

HA! I KNEW IT WAS YOU WHO TOOK MY SAFE, MUGWORT!

RICOTTA! LET'S SETTLE THIS ONCE AND FOR ALL!

SOCK!

THUD!

SMACK!

JUST A STONE'S THROW AWAY...

I'VE TIED THE ROPE TO THE SAFE! NOW DRIVE, "FINGERS", BUT SLOWLY!

OKAY, MICKEY!

VRRRRR!

AND...

GREAT! NOW DO YOUR STUFF "FINGERS"!

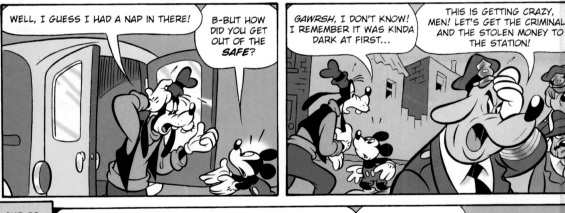

FALL IS HERE, AND ON THE SHORES OF LAKE LACUNA —

PAY ATTENTION, UNCA DONALD!

IT'S OUR SERVE NOW!

Walt Disney's
Donald Duck in
A RING FOR DONALD

H 85158

THE BALL'S GOING RIGHT TO YOU!

ALL YOU HAVE TO DO IS HIT IT BACK!

IT'LL BE A CINCH!

FLAP!

ARE YOU ALRIGHT, UNCA DONALD?

—:SIGH!:— I TOLD YOU KIDS IT WAS *NO USE* EVEN TRYING!

AW, COME ON! TRY AGAIN!

THAT WAS JUST AN UNFORTUNATE ACCIDENT!

IT DOESN'T MEAN A THING!

ALL RIGHT! ALL RIGHT! I'LL SERVE THE BALL!

POING!

UH-OH!

OOF!

I GIVE UP, BOYS! I'D BETTER GO BACK INSIDE... AND *STAY* THERE!

NO MAIL, EITHER!

RRRIP!

WATCH YOUR STEP! THERE'S THAT BOARD YOU CRASHED THROUGH YESTERDAY!

YEAH, I SEE IT!

WHAP!

⋲SOB!⋲

THE LONGER THIS BAD LUCK STREAK GOES ON, THE *WORSE* IT GETS!

AND IT WAS BAD ENOUGH BACK IN DUCKBURG WHEN DAISY JILTED HIM AND HE LOST FOUR JOBS IN THREE DAYS!

FACE IT, GUYS! WE'RE GONNA BE MAROONED OUT HERE UNTIL UNCA DONALD'S LUCK CHANGES...

...BECAUSE HE'S AFRAID OF WHAT MIGHT HAPPEN TO HIM IN A BUSY CITY! *ESPECIALLY* AFTER THAT INCIDENT WITH THE COAL TRUCK!

⋲SIGH!⋲ JUST THIRTY YEARS AGO, LAKE LACUNA WAS A BOOMING VACATION RESORT FOR THE RICH!

BUT NOW WE'RE THE ONLY ONES WHO EVER COME!

WHAT I WOULDN'T GIVE TO BE BACK IN DUCKBURG!

ME, TOO! WE'VE *GOT* TO DO SOMETHING TO GET UNCA DONALD BACK ON TRACK!

BUT WHAT? HIS PRIDE HAS TAKEN SUCH A BEATING...

IT WOULD TAKE A *MIRACLE* TO CHEER HIM!

HE'S SO DEPRESSED NOW, HE'S AFRAID TO TRY ANYTHING!

BUT IN LIFE, WHEN YOU KICK THE BALL AND YOU DON'T LIKE WHERE IT LANDS...

...YOU HAVE TO KICK IT *AGAIN!*

POOF!

SOMETHING *SHARP* WENT RIGHT THROUGH THE RUBBER!

HERE'S WHAT DID IT — AN *EXPENSIVE*-LOOKING *RING!*

LET ME SEE THAT!

WOW! THIS IS THE FAMOUS "TRINKETTO CORNUCOPIA"!!! THE HORN OF PLENTY, LOST FORTY YEARS AGO!

YEAH! THE GOOD LUCK CHARM WORN BY RUDOLPHO RAVISHINO, THE FAMOUS MOVIE STAR!

I BET *HE'D* LIKE TO GET IT BACK!

HE ALWAYS CREDITED THE RING FOR *HIS* SUCCESS!

BUT EVER SINCE HE LOST IT IN THIS LAKE BACK IN THE 60'S, HIS CAREER HAS GONE *NOWHERE!*

HE MIGHT GIVE US A BIG *REWARD!*

ENOUGH TO GET UNCA DONALD ON HIS FEET AGAIN!

WE'LL FINALLY BE ABLE TO GET HOME!

WHOA! LISTEN TO THIS...

...SUPPOSE *UNCA DONALD* WERE TO FIND THE RING AND RETURN IT? WOULDN'T THAT RESOLVE EVEN *MORE*?

YEAH! WE'D KILL *TWO* BIRDS WITH ONE PRECIOUS STONE!

IT WOULD SOLVE UNCA DONALD'S FINANCIAL *AND PSYCHOLOGICAL* PROBLEMS!

ALL WE HAVE TO DO IS *PLANT* THE RING SOMEWHERE AND LEAD HIM TO IT!

HOW ABOUT THAT HOLLOW TREE?

GREAT! AND AS FOR THE REST OF THE PLAN...

SOON —

I'D BETTER TAKE THIS NET DOWN! DON'T WANT ANY MORE ACCIDENTS!

OH, UNCA DONALD!

WE NEED YOUR HELP! HUEY LOST HIS CAP WHEN HE STUCK HIS HEAD INSIDE A HOLLOW TREE...

AND ONLY *YOUR* ARMS ARE LONG ENOUGH TO REACH IT!

HUEY'S CAP!

PLOCK!

WELL, IF I BEND OVER *FAR* ENOUGH...

NO CAP, BUT I FEEL SOMETHING *ELSE* IN THERE!

CRACK!

HERE'S AN OLD CAN OF RAT POISON, UNCA DON—

WE STUCK THE RING IN THERE! HE'LL FIND IT AS HE OPENS THE LID!

BETTER LET *ME* HANDLE THAT!

GRAB!

STEP ASIDE! WE CAN'T HAVE A SICK KID ON TOP OF EVERYTHING ELSE!

RAT POISO

IT'S UPSIDE DOWN!

FLOP!

THE RING! THE RING!

I SAW IT BOUNCE THAT WAY!

COFF! COFF!

OH NO! IT LANDED ON THE RAT'S TAIL!

CATCH HIM!

MUCH LATER —

YOU LOOK A *LITTLE* BETTER, UNCA DONALD! SOME OF THE *BLUE* HAS FADED FROM YOUR GREEN PALLOR!

WHEW! THERE'S LOUIE WITH THE RING!

—*PUFF! PUFF!*— CAUGHT HIM BEFORE HE DOVE INTO THE MARSH!

WE'RE GONNA HAVE TO START BEING MORE *OBVIOUS*, MEN!

YEAH?

WHAT DO YOU SUGGEST?

SO FAR, WE'VE TRIED TO LEAD UNCA DONALD TO THE RING! WHAT IF WE *REVERSED* THE PLAN...

...AND DANGLED IT IN FRONT OF HIS EYES SO HE *CAN'T* MISS IT!

FISHING!

SOON —

THIS WILL DO YOU A LOT OF GOOD, UNCA DONALD!

WHY SHOULD I BOTHER?

-*SIGH!*- WHAT CAN *I* EXPECT TO CATCH?

-*PSST!*- DO IT NOW!

THAT'S UNCA DONALD'S HOOK! THE ONE WITH THE *SMALL* WORM!

THIS CATCH WILL MAKE HIM SMILE... ALL THE WAY BACK TO DUCKBURG!

GLOM!

?

I GUESS SOME FISH *ARE* ATTRACTED TO GLITTERY OBJECTS, OH WELL!

IS THAT ALL I CAUGHT? BIG DEAL!

???

DON'T WORRY! AS SOON AS HE GETS THE FISH OFF THE HOOK, HE'LL SEE THE RING!

BOYS, AS SOON AS I TAKE CARE OF THIS MINNOW I WANT TO GO HOME! THIS HAS BEEN A COMPLETE WASTE OF TIME!

LA-LA-LAAA! THINGS ARE FINALLY LOOKING UP! A CLEAR SKY...

...NO WIND... AND THE LAKE IS AS FLAT AS GLASS!

NEED ANY HELP, UNCA DONALD?

YANK!
YANK!

LOOK AT THAT *FISH*!!!

WHAT A *WHOPPER*!

SOME CATCH!

WOW!

AIN'T THIS A *DREAM* OF A CATCH, UNCA DONALD?

OH, SURE...

HEY! WHERE'S YOUR FISHING POLE, AND... AND...

I THREW IT ALL INTO THE LAKE — WHAT ELSE?

YOU KIDS JUST SHOWED ME HOW *REAL* FISHING IS DONE!

GURGLE!

AND SO —

IN LIFE, WHEN YOU KICK THE BALL...

...AND SEE IT DISAPPEAR OVER THE FENCE...

...JUST AIM FOR THE NEXT BEST THING...

...AND KICK IT *REALLY GOOD*!!!

The End

Walt Disney's

Li'l Bad Wolf

in **The Great Hawk Hunt**

D 97308

LOOK AT THIS BABY BLUEBIRD I FOUND, POP! ISN'T SHE *CUTE?*

SO FATHER LOTS MOU...

IT'S SURE A SHAME HER LEG'S SPRAINED! SHE FELL OUTTA HER NEST!

DOUBLE BAH!

SHE'S AN *ORPHAN,* AND *I'M* TAKING *CARE* OF HER!

TRIPLE BAH!

NO SON O' *MINE'S* GROWIN' INTO A SQUAB-CUDDLIN' SISSY! YOU'RE GONNA BE A *BAD WOLF*-- DON'T FERGIT IT!

BLUEBIRDS IS FER *EATIN'!* IF YOU WARN'T A HOSPITAL CASE, SISTER, YOU'D GO IN TH' OVEN HERE AN' NOW!

B-BUT POP! I--

GIVE THIS BEAT-UP TWEET TO THEM THREE PIGS! LET *FOOD* RAISE *FOOD!* ⸱SNORT!⸱

IF YA GOTTA HAVE A BIRD FER A PET, SON, IT'LL BE TH' KIND A *REAL WOLF* KEEPS! WE'RE GOIN' HAWK HUNTING!

...AND CUB HIE TO THE HILLTOPS!

...A HAWKS LIVE ON DEMONTOOTH ...NTAIN! THAT'S 'CAUSE IT'S FULLA ...L TH' CRITTERS THEY LIKE TO *EAT!*

>GULP!< INCLUDING *WOLVES,* POP?

DON'T *FRET,* BOY!

US *PREDATORS* SEES *EYE-TO-EYE,* LI'L WOLF! FOR A HAWK, EATIN' *ME* 'UD BE LIKE EATIN' HIS *COUSIN!*

WELL, HERE COMES YOUR FAMILY REUNION!

yEEEEK!

OWF!

?!

SCRUNCH!!

HE'S *ORNERY* ENUFF FOR ME, BUT >OUCH!< WHY PROVE THAT *NOW?!*

BIFF!

SOCK!

CLOBBER!

PECK!

I THOUGHT YOU *SAW* EYE-TO-EYE WITH HAWKS!

I JUST *DID,* SON! FOR *THIRTY SECONDS TOO LONG!*

LET'S GO HOME, LI'L WOLF! I'VE HAD ENUFF EXERCISE FER ONE DAY!

BUT, POP!

WHAT ABOUT *CATCHING* THE HAWK?

ER

I'LL HAFTA *BREAK HIM IN* LIKE MOUNTAINEERS USETA DO WITH PACK MULES!

THE IDEA'S TO *GRAB 'IM AN'* HOLD 'IM *TIGHT* BEFORE HE KNOWS WHAT'S GOIN' ON!

GOTCHA! THIS *JUDO HOLD* OUGHTTA BE *TIGHT* ENUFF!

¿OWOOCH!¿ BUT IT OBVIOUSLY *AIN'T!*

PECK! GRIND! BLAT!

LET'S GO HOME! I'LL KEEP MY BLUEBIRD INSTEAD OF GIVING HER TO THE PIGS--

NO, YOU *WON'T!* THIS BUZZARD'S GOT ME *MAD!*

NOW I *GOTTA* KETCH HIM! IT'S A MATTER O' *HONOR!*

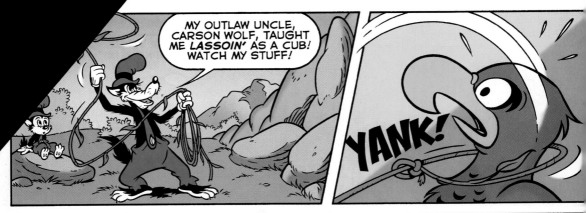

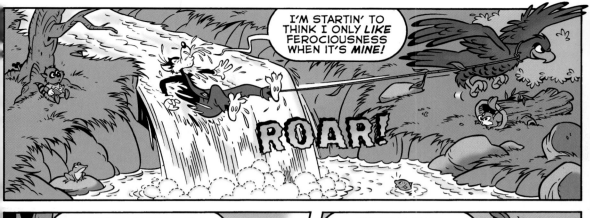

A FEW MINUTES LATER!

⁒GROAN!⁒ ME AND MY BRIGHT IDEAS!

IMAGINE HAVIN' THAT HAWK FER A PET! YEP, THERE SURE ARE FATES WORSE THAN DEATH...

AN' FACIN' MY SON IS ONE OF 'EM! I WON'T STAY A BAD ROLE MODEL FOR HIM IF I ADMIT I COULDN'T LICK THAT BIRDBRAIN!

AW, WELL! I JUST HAFTA FIB A LITTLE! LUCKY I'M GOOD AT IT!

HIYA, LI'L WOLF!

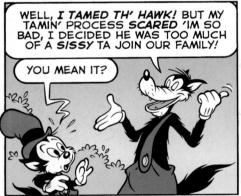

WELL, I TAMED TH' HAWK! BUT MY TAMIN' PROCESS SCARED 'IM SO BAD, I DECIDED HE WAS TOO MUCH OF A SISSY TA JOIN OUR FAMILY!

YOU MEAN IT?

HE DOESN'T LOOK LIKE A SISSY TO ME!

AS EVENING SHADOWS FALL!

YOU'LL BE A REAL WOLF'S BIRD YET! NOW GROWL!

CHEEEEP!

WINK!

The End

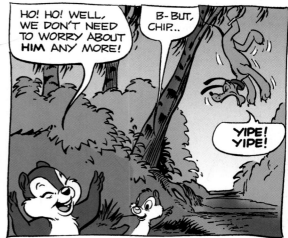

MISTER! MISTER! IF YOU WANT A SWELL PICTURE... COME QUICK!

A GOOD PICTURE? OH, BY ALL MEANS!

GO AHEAD! CLICK IT, MISTER!

CALL IT "CHIPMUNKS WIN AGAIN!"

WONDERFUL! THIS WILL BE A PRIZE PICTURE FOR SURE!

AND SO...SURE ENOUGH!

UNCLE MICKEY! LOOK!

LOOK AT THIS PICTURE THAT WON THE SNAPSHOT CONTEST IN THE NEWSPAPER!

WHY, IT'S PLUTO AND...

PLUTO! I WOULDN'T BELIEVE THIS IF I DIDN'T SEE IT WITH MY OWN EYES!

DAILY BUGLE
CAMERA CONTEST WINNER

CHIPMUNK CHAMPIONS

DO YOU MEAN YOU ACTUALLY LET LITTLE CHIPMUNKS BEAT UP ON YOU?

GULP!

I'M ASHAMED OF YOU, PLUTO! WHY... YOU'LL BE THE LAUGHING STOCK OF THE WHOLE TOWN!

AW! POOR GUY!

DON'T BLAME HIM, MISTER! HE COULDN'T HELP IT!

GOLLY, YES ...YA GOTTA REMEMBER...

...IT WAS TWO AGAINST ONE!

THE MOUNTAIN OF YOUTH!

It's all in here!

SpongeBob SquarePants, Toy Story, Superman, Jimmy Neutron, Spider-Man, Roy Rogers, Garfield, Uncle Scrooge, Buck Rogers, Pokemon, Small Soldiers, Superhero Resins, Batman, Muhammad Ali, The Lone Ranger, Disneyana, KISS, Mickey Mouse, Puppet Master, Elvis, The Phantom, X-Men, Charlie Chaplin, The Cisco Kid, Donald Duck, Captain Marvel, Laurel & Hardy, Howdy Doody, Planet of the Apes, MAD, Hopalong Cassidy, Captain America, Toy Guns and more! Many rare and one-of-a-kind collectibles are included in the new, expanded and updated listings.

OFFICIAL
Hake's Price Guide to **Character Toys**

All characters © 2004 respective copyright holders. All rights reserved.

This amazing photo volume contains!

Almost 15,000 items!

Almost 45,000 prices listed!

Every item is pictured!

More than 1,100 pages!

All-new color section!

Expanded and updated listings!

370 unique categories!

Checklist feature!

TO ORDER CALL SARA AT 888-375-9800 EXT. 410

For centuries, the elusive "fountain of youth" has been just beyond the realm of possibility, but now with the HAKE'S PRICE & PHOTO GUIDE TO CHARACTER TOYS #5, you can relive your childhood with the help of this all-in-one collectible guide! Stay young at heart with this mountainous volume packed with nostalgic pricing and pictures! HAKE'S PRICE GUIDE TO CHARACTER TOYS #5 - where youth springs eternal!

ALMOST 15,000 ITEMS SHOWN!

$35 +s&h

WALT DISNEY'S DONALD DUCK in "VIRTUALLY A HERO"

TAKE THAT...AND THAT... AND *THAT!*

BEEP! PLOOP!

WATCH OUT, YOU CRAZY DUCK!

KA-CHING! KWEE!

THWACK!

SORRY, I DIDN'T SEE YOU! I WAS PLAYING "SPACE MARAUDERS VII" AND I JUST REACHED THE *FINAL LEVEL!*

I'M THE *ONLY* COMPUTER GAME PLAYER IN DUCKBURG TO EVER GET THAT FAR! IT'S A SURE TICKET TO THE *WORLD CHAMPIONSHIPS!*

WORLD CHAMPIONSHIPS IN *VIDEO GAMES?* WHAT PLANET ARE *YOU* FROM?

LOOK! TH-TH-THAT'S OUR DUCK!

WELL, FROM WHAT HE SAYS, IT *SOUNDS* LIKE HE'S QUALIFIED, BUT —

NO BUTS! WE HAVEN'T GOT *TIME* TO FIND ANOTHER SUBJECT!

WAIT! IF HE *ISN'T* GOOD ENOUGH, IT COULD *KILL* HIM!

THAT CAN'T BE HELPED! THAT IS, UNLESS *YOU* WANT TO DO IT?!

→EEP!← N–N–NO! ON SECOND THOUGHT, HE'S *PERFECT!*

BUS STOP

SORRY! DIDN'T SEE YOU!

YOU THERE! PLEASE WAIT UP!

DO YOU WANT TO BE *REWARDED* BEYOND YOUR *WILDEST DREAMS*?

HUH? WHO *WOULDN'T*?!

OF COURSE, IT *DEPENDS* ON WHAT I HAVE TO *DO*!

JUST COME WITH US! WE'LL SHOW YOU A *VIDEO GAME* THAT WILL BE A *CHALLENGE* FOR EVEN AN EXPERT LIKE YOU!

SHORTLY —

THIS *EXPERIMENTAL VIRTUAL REALITY MACHINE* IS WHAT IT'S ALL ABOUT, MR. DUCK!

WE NEED A HIGHLY SKILLED PLAYER LIKE YOU TO *TEST* IT FOR US!

EXPERIMENTAL, YOU SAY? SOUNDS *DANGEROUS* TO ME!

OH, NO, MR. DUCK! THE *MACHINE* IS NOT DANGEROUS!

NOT IN THE SLIGHTEST! IT'S *100% SAFE!*

SEE? YOU JUST SIT IN THIS COMFY CHAIR AND WEAR OUR PRE-PROGRAMMED *VIRTUAL REALITY HELMET!*

IN THE GAME SCENARIO, YOU'LL PLAY THE ROLE OF THE INTERGALACTIC HERO, *SPACE RANGER!*

YOUR MISSION WILL BE TO SAVE THE BEAUTIFUL *PRINCESS DELISH*, WHO'S BEEN *KIDNAPPED* BY THE EVIL CONQUEROR *SCREEGO!*

SHE'S IMPRISONED ON THE *PLANET DREADMORE*, AND... WELL, YOUR HELMET MONITOR WILL FILL YOU IN ON THE... UM... *DETAILS!*

GEEZ! YOU GUYS HAVE THROWN IN EVERY *CLICHÉ* IN THE BOOK!

OH WELL, I'M ALWAYS *GAME* FOR A NEW GAME — AND GETTING *PAID* FOR PLAYING IS EVEN *BETTER!* BUT *HOW MUCH* DO YOU PAY?

DON'T WORRY! WE GUARANTEE THAT YOU'LL BE *WELL SATISFIED* WITH WHAT YOU GET!

BUT YOU'LL GET IT ONLY AFTER YOU *FINISH* THE GAME!

IF YOU FINISH IT!

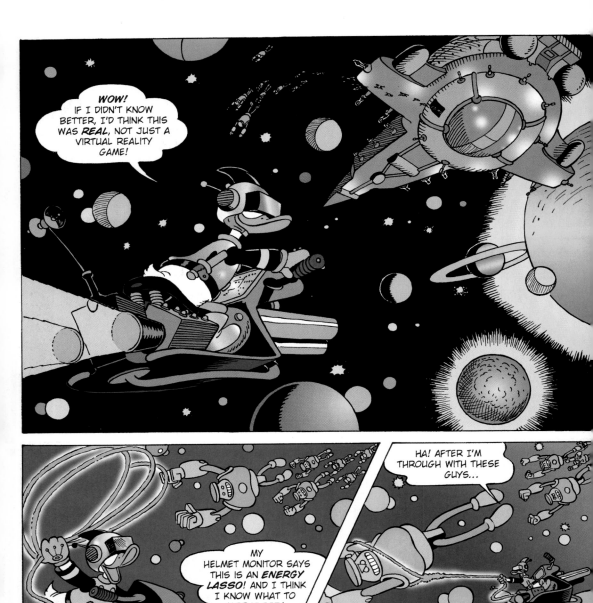

IT WON'T BE *ME*, THOUGH! I'LL BE TOO BUSY SAVING PRINCESS DELISH FROM THE CLUTCHES OF THE ROTTEN SCREEGO!

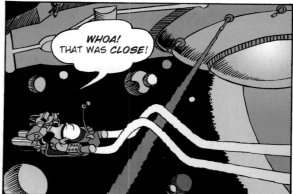

WHOA! THAT WAS *CLOSE!*

BUT IF SCREEGO THINKS I'M WORRIED ABOUT HIS *PUNY* LASER CANNONS, HE CAN THINK AGAIN!

STILL, I DON'T WANT TO WASTE TIME PLAYING *TAG* OUT HERE...

...SO I'LL USE ONE OF THE NIFTY LITTLE *GADGETS* LISTED IN MY SCOOTER'S EQUIPMENT INVENTORY!

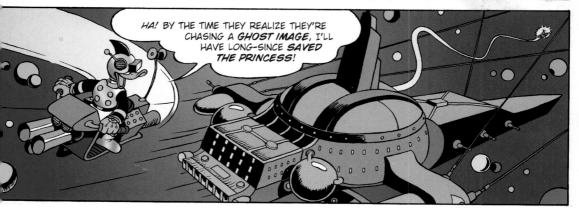

HA! BY THE TIME THEY REALIZE THEY'RE CHASING A *GHOST IMAGE*, I'LL HAVE LONG-SINCE *SAVED THE PRINCESS!*

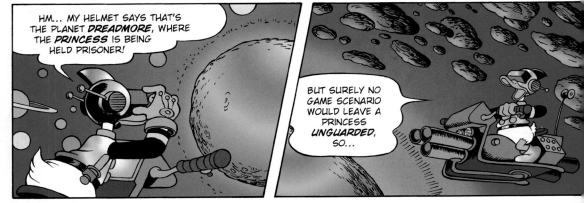

HM... MY HELMET SAYS THAT'S THE PLANET *DREADMORE*, WHERE THE *PRINCESS* IS BEING HELD PRISONER!

BUT SURELY NO GAME SCENARIO WOULD LEAVE A PRINCESS *UNGUARDED*, SO...

...MAYBE I'D BETTER NOT GO DOWN THERE *ALONE!*

COME ON, BOYS!

FOLLOW ME!

YE CATS! LOOKS LIKE THE PRINCESS IS *WELL-GUARDED!* THOSE ROBOT WAR MACHINES ARE *HUGE!*

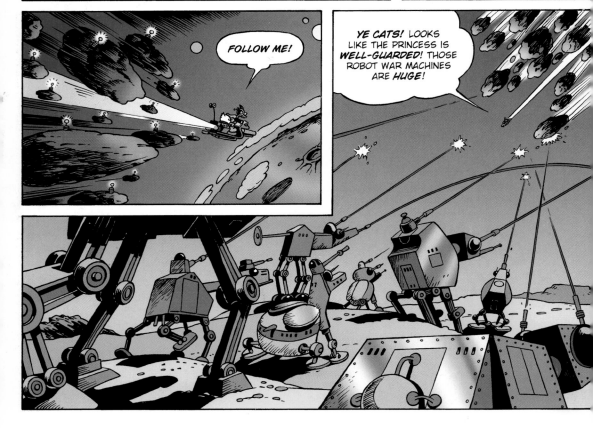

AT LAST! THEY SENT A **HERO** TO RESCUE ME!

-:SNARL!:-

-:GNASH!:-

-:DROOL!:-

-:EEK!:-

WHOOPS! LOOKS LIKE WE'LL HAVE TO **POSTPONE** THAT RESCUE A BIT!

DON'T WORRY, MY PRINCESS! I STILL HAVE A FEW MORE **TRICKS** UP MY SLEEVE!

ZAP!

ZAP!

BZZZT!

-:WHIMPER!:-

-:RIBBIT!:-

GOOD GRIEF! THIS IS GETTING **RIDICULOUS**!

ZAP!

WHAT HAVE YOU **DONE** TO HIM?

WHAT WE **HAD** TO DO TO **SAVE** YOU, YOUR HIGHNESS! YOU KNOW ALL OF YOUR **SUBJECTS** ARE TOO **COWARDLY** TO BE HEROES!

OUR ONLY CHANCE WAS TO FIND AN **EARTHLING**! THEY SEEM TO THINK DANGEROUS ADVENTURES ARE **FUN**!

→SIGH!← BUT WHY DIDN'T YOU JUST TELL THIS **BRAVE** DUCK THE **TRUTH** AND **ASK** HIM TO HELP?

WE... WE DIDN'T THINK ANYONE WOULD BE FOOLISH ENOUGH TO **VOLUNTEER** FOR **THIS** MISSION!

BESIDES, TELLING HIM IT WAS ONLY A GAME GAVE HIM THE **CONFIDENCE** HE NEEDED TO **SUCCEED**!

HEY!

I'VE HAD **ENOUGH** OF YOUR TRICKS — AND YOUR **INSULTS**! I WANT THE **REWARD** YOU PROMISED, AND I WANT TO GO HOME – **NOW**!

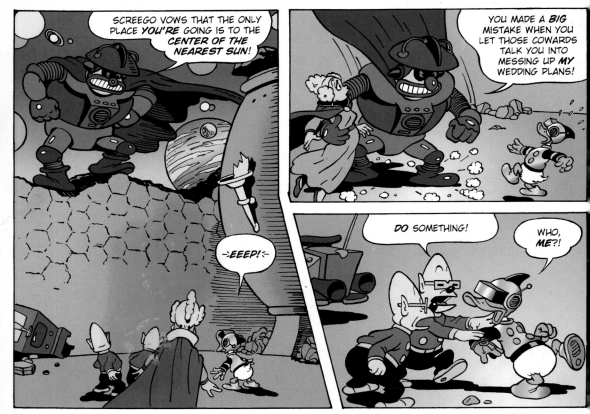

SCREEGO VOWS THAT THE ONLY PLACE **YOU'RE** GOING IS TO THE **CENTER OF THE NEAREST SUN**!

→EEEP!←

YOU MADE A **BIG** MISTAKE WHEN YOU LET THOSE COWARDS TALK YOU INTO MESSING UP **MY** WEDDING PLANS!

DO SOMETHING!

WHO, **ME**?!

WHAT DO YOU KNOW! I *DID* IT!

CRASH!

WHAT? WH-WHERE AM I?

OH! I'M SITTING IN THE VIRTUAL REALITY MACHINE!

I... I GUESS MY CLOBBERING SCREEGO WAS *ALSO* PART OF THE GAME!

~:GRRR!:~ SO WHERE ARE THOSE TWO *WEIRDOS* WHO HIRED ME? HIDING TO AVOID *PAYING* ME?

!!!

FLASH!

BUT... BUT... BUT IT WAS JUST A *GAME*...

OUR THANKS FOR YOUR HEROIC DEEDS!

PRINCESS DELISH

...WASN'T IT?

WALT DISNEY'S THE BEAGLE BOYS in BEST LAID PLANS

THIS TIME WE HAVE A PLAN THAT CAN'T FAIL!

WE ALWAYS SEEM TO MISS *SOMETHING* WHEN WE PLAN ON ROBBIN' OL' SCROOGE!

BUT *NOT* TODAY!

WE'VE MAPPED OUT *EVERY* POSSIBLE DETAIL OF OUR SCHEME!

D 98358

HONEST PEOPLE DON'T WORK HALF AS HARD AS WE HAVE, PLANNING THIS HEIST!

OKAY! 1:40 PM! IT'S TIME FOR PHASE ONE! YOU ALL KNOW WHAT TO DO?!

YEP!

AYE-AYE!

STEP NUMBER ONE... WE GO TO THE HARDWARE STORE FOR A DRILL FOR THE LOCK AND A ROPE TO TIE MCDUCK!

CHECK!

OPEN

WILL THAT BE ALL FOR TODAY?

YES! THANKS!

STEP NUMBER TWO... DYNAMITE, FROM THE FARM SUPPLY STORE, TO BLOW UP THE VAULT DOOR!

MUSTN'T FORGET THAT!

FARM SU

GRAIN

PITCHFORKS $5.00

GIVE US *LOTS* O DYNAMITE, PLEASE! WE GOT US A *BIG* STUMP TO BLAST!

YEAH! IT'S REAL *STUBBORN!*

ALL RIGHT, BOYS!

DYNAMITE

WHAT NEXT? AH, YES... THE *TRAVEL AGENCY!*

THE PLAN

GREETINGS, LADY! WE HAVE BEEN WORKING AWFUL HARD AND WANT PLANE TICKETS TO TAHITI!

HAR HAR!

TRAVEL DESK

HAWAII

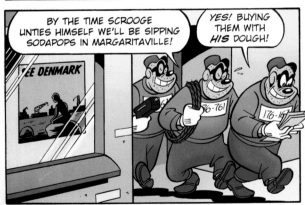

BY THE TIME SCROOGE UNTIES HIMSELF WE'LL BE SIPPING SODAPOPS IN MARGARITAVILLE!

YES! BUYING THEM WITH *HIS* DOUGH!

EE DENMARK

ALL RIGHT! LASTLY, STEP FOUR... A VISIT TO THE COSTUME SHOP!

RAVEL GENCY

MASQUERA SHOP

COSTUMES FOR ALL OCCASIO

HE-HE-HE! I *LOVE* A PLAN THAT GOES SMOOTHLY!

GAS

OK! WE'RE READY TO *ROLL!*

YEAH! IN MCDUCK'S *CASH!*

DYNAMITE

GAS

COSTUME RE

PHONE REPAIR

ANOTHER DYNAMIC DUO!

Shazam! ™ & ©2004 DC Comics, Inc. Donald Duck ™ & ©2004 Disney Enterprises. Overstreet® is a Registered Trademark of Gemstone Publishing, Inc. All rights reserved.

IT'S THE COMIC PAIR WITH PRICING FLAIR!

All the info you need about pricing your comics is right here in *The Official Overstreet® Comic Book Price Guide #34.* So, don't let your collection flounder - price it with panache using

THE ONE AND ONLY GUIDE!

COMIC SHOP LOCATOR SERVICE
888-COMIC-BOOK
888-266-4226

$25 +s&h

Call Sara at 888-375-7500 ext 410 to order!